MOVERS & SHAKERS

Classroom activities for elementary and intermediate students

Robin Price

DELTA PUBLISHING

ENGLISH TEACHING professional

ENGLISH TEACHING *professional*

Published by First Person Publishing Limited
12 Kent Road Chiswick, London W4 5EZ
and DELTA Publishing, 39 Alexandra Road,
Addlestone, Surrey KT15 2PQ

First published 1998

ISBN 0 953 30980 0

Photocopying

Pages marked:

(**DESIGNED TO PHOTOCOPY**)

Edited by Caroline Burke

Designed by Trevor Sylvester (TSGD)

Printed in Britain by Hillman Printers

Acknowledgements

Earlier versions of the following activities have appeared in ENGLISH TEACHING *professional*:

Pulp fiction	- Issue 2 (January 1997)
Streetwise	- Issue 3 (April 1997)
A blast from the past	- Issue 4 (July 1997)
Sue me!	- Issue 5 (October 1997)

The publisher would like to thank Roger Hunt, International House, London for his help in piloting activities.

Author acknowledgements

Special thanks to Nicolas Ridley, and the Westminster Two (Amanda and Doreen). Dedicated to Michele.

Contents

Note
The level that is indicated suggests the minimum level required for students to be able to deal with the activity productively and enjoyably, e.g. elementary+ indicates elementary and upwards.

1   Here comes trouble!

Level	elementary+
Time	40 minutes
Activity	split reading/dialogue building/role-play
In this lesson	an enjoyable activity based on a 'no win' situation generates the language of apologising, breaking bad news or avoiding the truth.

Teaching instructions

1 Pre-teach the following vocabulary:

   bowl; scream; mother-in-law; jewellery; bracelet; shade (of green); a no win situation (idiom); bump.

2 Tell your class that they are going to read about two embarrassing situations that a woman called Jane had to deal with. Make sure that your class understand the idea of 'embarrassment'. You could tell your own embarrassing story (e.g. you are about to pay for dinner at a restaurant when you discover that you have left all your money at home).

3 Divide the class into pairs and give out copies of A and B.

4 Students must read their own text and then answer their partner's questions.

5 While they are reading, write the following dialogues on the board:

   A Neighbour: 'Hi, we're back. We had a great holiday, I hope Tom was no problem?'
   Jane: 'Tom? Oh yes …'

   B Jane: 'Have another piece of cake dear.'
   Mother-in-law: 'Thank you darling. Why aren't you wearing your bracelet?'

6 Divide the class into small groups.

7 Tell them to use their imaginations and continue the dialogues, writing down what they think the people might say.

8 When they have had about fifteen minutes to work on their dialogues, get all the groups to read out their dialogues to the rest of the class.

9 If your class are confident, get them to role-play their dialogues. This gives you a good chance to work on their intonation.

10 Organise a group discussion based on the question:

   What's the most embarrassing situation you have ever been in?

A Cat trouble

We always had a good relationship with our neighbours.
When they asked us to look after their cat, called Tom,
for the weekend, I agreed to help. On Friday night I
let Tom into our kitchen. I gave him some cat food
and a big bowl of cream. On Saturday morning I was
very busy because I had to take the children to the
swimming pool. We got up early and as I drove the
car out of the garage, I felt something strange. There was
a bump, a horrible scream and then silence. Then I realised
that something terrible had happened. What should I tell
my neighbours?

Ask your partner these questions about his/her story.

1 Why did Jane receive the bracelet?
2 Why was it special?
3 Why did the bracelet change colour?
4 What is a 'no win' situation?
5 What would you do if you were Jane?

Cut here ✂ -

B The birthday present

I love jewellery so I was delighted when my mother-in-law
gave me a beautiful, gold bracelet for my birthday. She said
it was made of a special antique gold — over a hundred
years old. She had bought the bracelet from a department
store when she was in London. I loved the bracelet and
I wore it all the time. Sometimes I even forgot to take
it off in the shower. Every Sunday the family had dinner
together. My mother-in-law always talked about the bracelet.
She said that gold made me look so beautiful. One Sunday
morning my husband said, 'What's wrong with your bracelet?'
When I looked down, I noticed that the gold had changed
colour, to a strange shade of green! I was in a no win
situation. What should I say to my mother-in-law?

Ask your partner these questions about his/her story.

1 Who was Tom?
2 Why was Jane looking after Tom?
3 Why was she busy on Saturday morning?
4 What was the terrible thing that happened?
5 What would you do if you were Jane?

2 Moral maze

Level	intermediate
Time	40 minutes
Activity	retelling a story/discussion
In this lesson	as well as practising the second conditional, this activity generates the language of speculation and can lead to a lively discussion

Teaching instructions

1 Pre-teach the following vocabulary:

   serial number; to stare at; drawer; to fail; headmaster; to make a speech; a strict vegetarian.

2 Divide the class into groups of four and give each student within the group a different story. If you cannot divide your class exactly into groups of four students you can always make one or two groups of three students and give them their final story (D) to read at the end of the activity.

3 Students should read their own story and tell it to the other students in the group (with their own text covered up).

4 When all the stories have been told, tell the group to exchange stories to check that they have fully understood them.

5 Tell each group to write down what they would do in that situation. Do some class feedback to find out which situation presents the biggest moral dilemma.

A Stolen goods

Grant and Anya had just got married. One of the most expensive wedding gifts that they got was a video camera, from Grant's brother Phil. Grant was surprised because Phil wasn't rich. It was a really good quality video camera. It must have cost at least £700. Two weeks later Grant had another surprise. He was watching a programme called *Catch the Criminal* on television. Some thieves had broken into an electronics shop and stolen some video cameras. Grant was worried when he saw a picture of one of the stolen cameras; it looked exactly the same as his wedding present! He checked the serial number on his video camera and he found that it had been stolen.

Cut here --

B Love letters

It's rude to read other people's mail, but when I saw the letters on the desk I couldn't resist having a look. My sister wanted me to look after her flat while she and her husband went on holiday. I was tidying up when I found the letters. There were more than fifteen of them in the bottom drawer. As soon as I read the first page, I realised that they were love letters. They were to Richard, but not from my sister! The last letter had been written just two weeks ago.

Cut here --

C Test of honesty

My son was sixteen years old. He was studying hard, but he was sure that he was going to fail an important mathematics exam. His teacher, Mrs Kono had told him that he would never pass. I was working as a cleaner at his school. I was in the headmaster's office one morning when I found a document on the floor. I picked it up and looked at it. The title read: *Mathematics examination answers, class 6, teacher: Mrs Kono.* I just didn't know what to do. Should I photocopy the answers to help my son?

Cut here --

D Vegetarian surprise

My boss, Mr Santana, had invited some special customers to his house for dinner. He invited me too. When I arrived, he made a speech, telling everyone to enjoy themselves. I was next to Mr Klein, the most important guest. We were sitting opposite my boss's wife. Mrs Santana had spent ages preparing a special meal. When she brought the food in, I found that she'd cooked a roast beef dinner. She must have forgotten that I'm a strict vegetarian! In a loud voice, Mr Klein asked me why I wasn't eating. Everyone stared at me.

Where do you stand?

Level	intermediate+
Time	55 minutes
Activity	discussion/writing speeches
In this lesson	vocabulary and expressions relating to politics are introduced and the activity generates the language of agreement and disagreement.
Warning!	this exercise can reveal strong opinions so it is recommended for groups that can enjoy a lively discussion without taking offence.

Teaching instructions

1 If your class have not discussed political issues before, they will find that there is a lot of new vocabulary in this lesson. Keywords in the statements have been defined in a glossary, but lower-level classes will probably need some extra help. With lower-level or less confident classes, go through the vocabulary in the glossary, making sure that everyone understands the concepts, before you give out the statements.

2 Make sure that everyone understands the idea of the political spectrum (left to right).

3 Divide the class into small groups and give out the statements.

4 Tell your students to work through the list of statements, deciding whether they are left-wing or right-wing views.

5 When they have finished, tell each student to select three statements that he/she agrees with and another three statements that he/she disagrees with.

6 Combine the groups so that there are about four to six people in each group. Tell the students to compare their results and explain why they agree or disagree with the statements.

7 Tell the groups to write four to six new statements of their own (depending on the size of the group).

8 Get the different groups to compare their new statements and discuss them.

Here are some political statements. Are they the views of:

a) people on the right

b) people on the left

c) both/neither.

1 The rich are getting richer and the poor are getting poorer.
2 Companies that pollute the environment should pay to clean up their mess.
3 There will always be trouble between workers and bosses.
4 Tax is too high in this country.
5 The unemployed are lazy, they should be forced to join the army.
6 The family is the most important group in society.
7 Hospitals and schools should be free for everyone to use.
8 Fathers should go out to work and mothers should stay at home and look after the children.
9 Capital punishment stops people from committing crimes like murder.
10 There's no such thing as an honest politician.
11 War is wrong for any reason, and selling arms is wrong too.
12 It's wrong to test cosmetic products like shampoo on animals.
13 It's always wrong to break the law.
14 There are too many foreigners in this country.
15 Whales have always been hunted, no one should stop this happening.

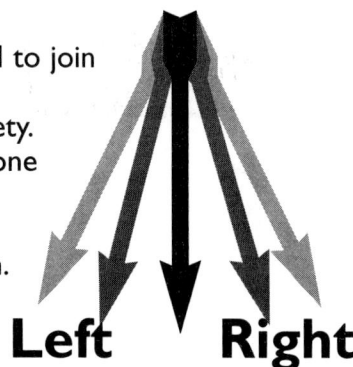

Left   Right

Keywords	
arms	weapons like tanks, aircraft, guns or bombs
capital punishment	the death sentence
to commit a crime	to do something illegal
foreigners	people from another country
to hunt	to chase after an animal and kill it
management	people who control a business (i.e. bosses or employers)
to pollute	to damage the environment with harmful substances like chemicals or oil
tax	money collected by the government
to test something (on animals)	to experiment with a new product to find out if it is safe for humans to use
the unemployed	people who don't have jobs

4 A blast from the past

Level	elementary+
Time	40 minutes
Activity	reading/inventing scenarios/discussion
In this lesson	the rules for adjectives ending in -ed/-ing are revised. A problem solving activity generates the language of making suggestions, agreeing and disagreeing.

Teaching instructions

1 Give out copies of Part 1 and tell students to work in pairs, adding words to the lists in Exercise 1.

2 When they have finished, elicit the words they have chosen and write them on the board in two long lists.

3 In Exercise 2 students have to fill in the gaps with adjectives.

4 When they have finished, go through the answers to Exercise 2, revising the rules for adjectives ending in -ed/ing in the grammar check box.

   Answers
   1 e   2 a   3 b   4 c   5 d

5 Discuss the sentences.

6 Divide the class into small groups and give them a copy of Part 2.

7 Tell the groups to read the problems (A–C) and decide what they would do in each situation.

8 Ask the groups to report back and compare solutions around the class.

9 Now split the whole class into three groups.

10 Tell each group to think up one or more 'problem situation(s)' from the past and write them down.

11 Now you are ready to play the game. Group A has to explain a 'problem situation' and Groups B and C have to suggest solutions. Group A gives a point to the group with the best answer to their problem. Repeat the process until you have run out of problems.

A blast from the past   4

Part 1

1 Work with a partner. Add five words to these lists about life in the past.

Three hundred years ago they didn't have: cars, McDonald's, advanced medicine ....
Three hundred years ago they had: horses, feasts, swords
....

2 Fill in the gaps using a word from the box. Do you agree with the statements?

> a) amazing   b) terrified   c) charming
> d) depressed   e) exhausting

1 Life was really tough. People woke up at sunrise and went to sleep feeling tired after an .... day in the fields.
2 Kings and queens had an .... life and enough money to buy anything.
3 Because they didn't understand science, many people were .... of things like thunder and lightening.
4 In the old days, life was better for women because men had to be ....
5 Nobody felt .... because stress didn't exist.

Grammar check
adjectives ending in -ed and -ing

Many adjectives end in -ed, for example, *bored, interested, disappointed*. These are used to talk about our feelings, for example, *I was bored yesterday*. Other adjectives end with the letters -ing, for example, *boring, interesting, disgusting*, and *disappointing*. These describe events or experiences, for example, *The film was boring*.

Cut here ✂ -

Part 2

A You go riding in the woods, your friend falls off his horse and breaks his leg. You try to help him walk, but it's getting dark, you're exhausted and he's frightened and in terrible pain. Unfortunately, the year is 1680 and there are no hospitals, anaesthetics or telephones.

B You live in a small country town. The year is 1750. You are bored. Unfortunately, the television has not been invented yet and there are no radios or video recorders. How can you make your evenings more exciting?

C You are a highly intelligent person. You love studying and your family has enough money to send you to a good university. You're depressed because you'd like to study to be a doctor but unfortunately it is 1890 and women are not allowed at university.

5 Famous diaries

Level	elementary+
Time	45 minutes
Activity	discussion/reading/creative writing/guessing-game
In this lesson	lower-level classes can have fun with a guessing-game activity that also develops their vocabulary of likes and dislikes. Higher-level students will enjoy producing more detailed extracts from famous people's diaries.

Teaching instructions

1   Give out Part 1. Divide your class into pairs and tell them to match the people on the left with the descriptions on the right.

   Answers
   1 e   2 b   3 f   4 a   5 d   6 c

2   When they have finished tell them to decide whether these people are real or fictional.

3   Tell them to make two lists:

   a) the most famous people in my country
   b) the most famous people in the world

   In pairs students should compare their lists.

4   Before you give out the diary extracts in Part 2, you might prefer to pre-teach the following vocabulary:

   appalling; depressing; confusing; terrible; rotten; boring; fascinating; disgusting.

5   Divide the class into groups of three and give a different extract to each group.

6   You might like to explain the references e.g. 'There's something rotten about living in Denmark' (after 'something is rotten in the state of Denmark' from Shakespeare's *Hamlet*) but try not to give away the identity of the diary writers at this stage.

7   Within their groups discuss who might have written their extract.

8   Finally, tell your students to choose a famous person from history and write an extract from their diary (approximately 70–100 words).

9   Students from another group must guess the identity of the famous people.

Part 1

1 Napoleon	a) the first President of the USA
2 Sherlock Holmes	b) a famous detective, very clever
3 Columbus	c) she was a famous nurse
4 George Washington	d) he stole from the rich and gave to the poor
5 Robin Hood	e) a French emperor, also a great soldier
6 Florence Nightingale	f) the first European sailor to find America

Cut here ✂ -

Part 2   **A**

Dear Diary

Oh dear! The weather is appalling and this London fog

is terrible. I met Dr Watson at the club yesterday.

His story was so confusing. Fascinating case but

I still don't know who stole the wallet. That old

fool probably lost it anyway! I must buy some

more tobacco. Now, where did I put that violin?

Cut here ✂ -

B

Dear Diary

Life here in Sherwood forest is so boring. I'm tired of stealing things just
to buy beautiful new dresses and jewellery for Marian. If I don't come
home with a new dress or diamond ring she looks really disappointed.
And then there's the poor people. Why do they always expect me to give
them all the money we steal? If they want to get money why don't they
go to the forest and rob the rich like everyone else?

Cut here ✂ -

C

Dear Diary

It's so depressing here in this old castle. It's cold,
grey and sad. There's something rotten about
living here in Denmark. My mother gets on my
nerves. Getting married so soon after the death
of my father, it's disgusting! And her second
husband is a real idiot! To be or not to be?
That is the question. But what is the answer?

6 Doomed!

Level	intermediate+
Time	40 minutes
Activity	exchanging stories/inventing scenarios/report writing/discussion
In this lesson	as well as providing free practice of future tenses, this lesson generates speculative language in a debate on the end of the world.
Warning!	in any lesson dealing with a topic like 'Doomsday', discussion might develop that touches on religious issues. If you or members of your class are sensitive about religious issues or would feel uncomfortable discussing them - this is probably not the lesson for you.

Teaching instructions

1 Pre-teach the following vocabulary:

   hens; meteor; the devil.

2 Ask your class if they have heard of Doomsday (the day when the world comes to an end).

3 Divide the class into groups of four and give each student within the group a different story. Students should read their own story and tell it to the other people in their group (with their text covered up).

4 When all the stories have been told, tell each group to decide which stories are true and which are false.

   Answers
   A true   B true   C true   D false

5 While the students are busy reading their texts, write the following question on the board:

   How and when do you think the world will end?

6 Tell the groups to discuss this question and write a short report (70–100 words) on 'Doomsday' to be presented to the rest of the class. Here are a few suggestions: environmental Doomsday; Third World War; a UFO attack; a new kind of killer disease; global warming/new ice age.

7 A spokesperson from each group should read out their group's Doomsday report.

8 Organise a class discussion, ending in a vote to decide whose Doomsday theory is the most convincing.

   Variation - if you are pressed for time, set the Doomsday question as a composition title.

A There have been a lot of interesting predictions about Doomsday, probably the most famous one of all is in the book of Revelation, the very last book in the Bible. It says that the devil will come to the earth and everything will be destroyed. If you are worried about this happening, there is some good news and some bad news. The good news is that the lucky people will survive. The bad news is that only 144,000 people will make it!

Cut here ✂ -

B A lot of people have predicted the end of the world and then got it wrong. But very few people have ever said sorry for making a mistake. A group of Christians in America in the nineteenth century were led by a man called Miller. They predicted that the world would end in 1843. When 1843 came, the group got excited. The world didn't end, but Miller wasn't embarrassed about his mistake. Instead of saying sorry, Miller said, 'I got it wrong, the world is going to end next year in 1844'. 1844 came and went, but nothing happened. The group were so upset that they called that time 'The Great Disappointment'.

Cut here ✂ -

C In the 1800s in Britain, there was a poor woman called Mary Bateman. She had some hens. One day she claimed that her hens were laying magic eggs. The eggs had writing on them that said 'the end of the world is coming!' Some people were terrified, because they took Mary Bateman very seriously. She started charging people a penny to come and look at these amazing hens. The government was worried about her because she was making a lot of money out of the eggs. So they went to her house early one morning. They were surprised to find her writing on an egg and pushing it up a hen's bottom!

Cut here ✂ -

D Bernard McVicker was horrified when he dreamed that a giant meteor was going to crash into the earth. He was sure that the world was going to end on 4 July 1978. He wrote to the newspapers and walked through the streets telling people about the danger, but nobody believed his story. Finally, a local television station called and asked him to come and talk about the end of the world. Unfortunately his taxi crashed into a bus on the way to the television station. Bernard McVicker died in hospital on 4 July 1977.

7 Good causes

Level	elementary+
Time	50 minutes
Activity	reading/planning an event/designing a poster
In this lesson	students work in groups to plan their own charity events. This activity practises the language of advertising and persuading.

Teaching instructions

1   Pre-teach the following vocabulary:

to watch your figure; sponsored parachute jump; massive; huge; famine victims.

2   Divide the class into pairs and give out Part 1.

3   Now tell your class to look at the list of charities. What work do they do?

Answers
Amnesty International (human rights)
WWF (nature and the environment)
OXFAM (helps famine victims/developing countries)
Greenpeace (environmental pressure group)
Cancer Research (medical)

4   Tell them to make a list of other charities and suggest some more ways that charities raise money. Write these on the board.

5   Give out Part 2. Students must match the newspaper headlines with the stories.

Answers
1 C   2 B   3 D   4 A

6   Go over the answers, explaining any new vocabulary. Make sure that the class understand the idea of getting publicity for a charity by organising a special event or stunt (charity stunts are unusual events, designed to attract a lot of publicity).

7   Tell each group to write three newspaper headlines that publicise stunts/events for different charities.

8   Students read out their headlines to another group, who must guess:

a) which charity it is talking about
b) what the stunt is.

Good causes

Part 1

What do these charities do?

Amnesty International	WWF	OXFAM
Greenpeace	Cancer Research	

Cut here ✂ -

Part 2

A Seventeen year-old fashion model Susan Heart raised £260 for Greenpeace yesterday. She joined seven other workers at the local hairdresser's in a pasta eating competition. 'I ate six bowls of pasta in ten minutes,' claimed Susan. 'But now I'm on a diet and I have to watch my figure!'

B Professional baseball star Justin Banks joined the campaign to help the children of Los Angeles. He and the other members of his team joined in a sponsored parachute jump this weekend.

C Local women's rugby champion Jane Duff has spent the last six months growing vast vegetables. The massive carrots, giant potatoes and huge leaks were sold at the town hall yesterday. All the money will go to leukaemia (cancer of the blood).

D The night was full of stars yesterday when many famous faces were seen at a special party. Star guests included top radio DJ Steve Smash. Tickets for the meal cost £100 per person. The money will help famine victims in Africa.

Match the newspaper headlines with the stories.

1 CHAMPION HAS A LEAK FOR LEUKAEMIA

2 JUMP! JUSTIN TIME TO SAVE THE CHILDREN

3 MUSIC STARS EAT TO END WORLD HUNGER

4 MODEL SLURPS SPAGHETTI TO STOP SUFFERING

8   Road rage

Level	intermediate
Time	60 minutes
Activity	vocabulary building/split reading/dialogue building
In this lesson	students revise vocabulary relating to cars. Confident classes will enjoy the 'road rage' role-play.

Teaching instructions

1   Draw the outline of a car on the board. Ask your class to draw pictures of their own. Copy these words onto the board:

    boot; wipers; tyres; headlights; bonnet; wing mirror; windscreen; wheels; bumper.

2   Get the class to label their pictures with the words on the board.

3   Check their answers.

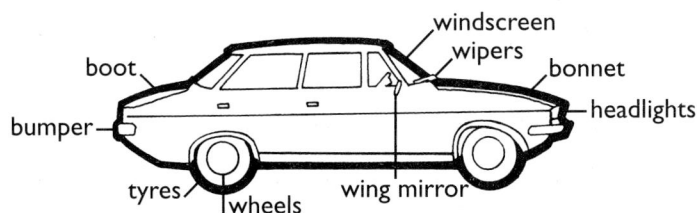

4   Before you give out copies of A and B, make sure that your class understand the idea of 'road rage' (drivers losing their tempers and behaving aggressively).

5   Divide the class into pairs and give out copies of A and B.

6   Students must read their own text and then answer their partner's questions.

7   While they are reading, write this dialogue on the board:

    Sarah: 'Hi Will, are you OK? You look a bit upset.'
    Will: 'Er, well, Sarah, there's been a bit of an accident ...'

8   Divide the class into small groups. Explain that Will is the 'road rage' driver from Text A and Sarah is his girlfriend. Tell the groups to use their imagination and continue the conversation, writing down what they think the people might say.

9   When they have had about fifteen minutes' preparation time, get the groups to read out (or act out) their dialogues to the rest of the class.

A Smashing driver

A 'road rage' driver smashed up his own car with a baseball bat after hitting a school bus this morning. 'You hear a lot about road rage these days, but I've never seen anything like that before,' said bus driver Neil Brown. A yellow Ford Sierrta estate crashed into the back of Mr Brown's bus just after 9.00 a.m. 'The driver got out of the car, opened the boot and took out a baseball bat. I was really worried. I thought he was going to attack me,' said Mr Brown. 'But he started smashing up his own car with the baseball bat. He was screaming and shouting and smashing the windscreen. 'I didn't think that asking him for his insurance details would have been a very good idea', Mr Brown added.

Ask your partner these questions:

1 What is road rage?
2 How common is road rage?
3 What is tailgating?
4 According to the report, what causes road rage?

Cut here ✂ -

B Mad person + car = mad driver

According to a new survey, 9 out of 10 people claim to have experienced 'road rage' and 6 out of 10 say that they've lost their temper whilst driving. The report also reveals that 1 person in every 100 claims that they've been the victim of a physical attack whilst driving. More common types of 'road rage' include: headlight flashing, verbal abuse, obscene gestures and aggressive driving like 'tailgating' (where drivers deliberately drive too close to the car in front to try to make the other driver speed up). So what causes bad behaviour like this? The survey outlines two theories. The first theory states that there's something about the stress of driving in heavy traffic that makes people extremely aggressive. The second theory argues that because society is becoming more and more violent, there are lots of crazy people on the roads.

Ask your partner these questions:

1 What is Mr Brown's job?
2 Describe the road rage incident.
3 Why was Mr Brown surprised?
4 Why didn't Mr Brown speak to the driver?

9 Yes, Mr President

Level	intermediate+
Time	50 minutes
Activity	role-play/discussion/speech writing
In this lesson	students are introduced to vocabulary relating to political and economic issues.

Teaching instructions

1   Before you start, you should make sure that your class are familiar with the policies listed in the information for Students B and C (health, tax, defence etc). To do this, ask your class, 'What do politicians often talk about?' Try to elicit a similar list and write it on the board. Go through the new vocabulary. Students will have to understand the idea of 'policies' that will win them votes in an election i.e. tax cuts, longer prison sentences for criminals etc.

2   Divide the class into groups of three. In each group you should have:

Student A   =   Robert Davies
Students B and C =   political advisors

3   Students should read their texts.

4   Students B and C need about ten minutes to think up their policies. These can be as serious or silly as they like. While they are planning, Student A should be thinking up more questions for them.

5   Role-play: the advisors meet Robert Davies. He asks his questions and they present him with his five key policies.

6   Writing an election speech: Tell each group that Robert has decided to run for president. The whole group must write a short election speech for him (approximately 100 words). Remind them to include the policies that they discussed earlier. A spokesperson from each group should read their group's speech. The class can vote to decide who to elect.

Robert Davies is a well-known actor. He is now 65 years old. He went to a party last night and one of his friends suggested that he tried to become a politician. Everyone thought it was a great idea! Unfortunately, Robert knows nothing at all about politics. A friend has asked Robert to meet a team of political advisors who can help him with his new career.

Cut here ✂ -

A You are *Robert Davies*. When you were young everybody loved your films. Now you want a career in politics. Unfortunately you have a bad memory. Last night you started to write a list of questions about politics. You didn't finish the list, but you made some notes at the bottom. Think of some extra questions to ask. Here are some examples:

1 How can I become president?
2 Can I buy votes?
3 Should I go on television?
4 What should I say?
5 What shouldn't I say?
6 What are the best policies on the environment, taxes, education etc?

Cut here ✂ -

B+C You are *political advisors*. Your boss has just told you that in ten minutes' time you will have a meeting with Mr Robert Davies (the famous actor). Your boss said that Robert looks good on television and has a great personality. The only problem is that he doesn't know much about politics. He wants to know which policies will be popular with the voters.

The economy	Trade	Crime	Drug control
Foreign policy	Transport	Defence	Education
Equal opportunities	Healthcare	Tax	The family
The environment	Immigration	Gambling	Spending

1 Look at the topics above and choose five that you think will be popular.

2 Invent simple policies for the five topics. Try to think of policies that will be popular with the voters. Here are some examples:

Trade	more trade with other countries is needed.
Education	more money should be spent on schools and universities.
Crime	crime is increasing so we'll build a hundred new prisons.

10 Food fun

Level	elementary
Time	40 minutes
Activity	reading/discussion/writing a recipe
In this lesson	an enjoyable activity generates discussion and develops vocabulary relating to food.

Teaching instructions

1 Divide your class into small groups. Write the alphabet on the board and get your students to write it out on a separate piece of paper. Give them five minutes to try to come up with as many types of food as possible and make a list (A=apple, B=bread etc).

2 Get some group feedback and write everybody's vocabulary on the board.

3 Give out Exercise 1. Students have to read the recipes, guess the names of the dishes or drinks and identify where they come from.

4 Go over the answers.

   Answers
1	cappuccino	(Italy)
2	sushi	(Japan)
3	hamburger	(USA)
4	paella	(Spain)
5	sweet and sour pork	(China)
6	fish and chips	(UK)

5 Make sure that students understand the idea of national or regional specialities.

6 Tell each student in the group to draw a rough map of their country (or their region in a monolingual class). Write the following on the board:

   a) List three special meals that are famous in your country/region.
   b) Which types of food are produced in your country/region? Mark them on your map.

7 When they have finished, students should compare their maps with the others in their group. Ask them to describe how the different dishes are made, (or write recipes like the examples).

8 Go round the class and find out which recipes are the most popular.

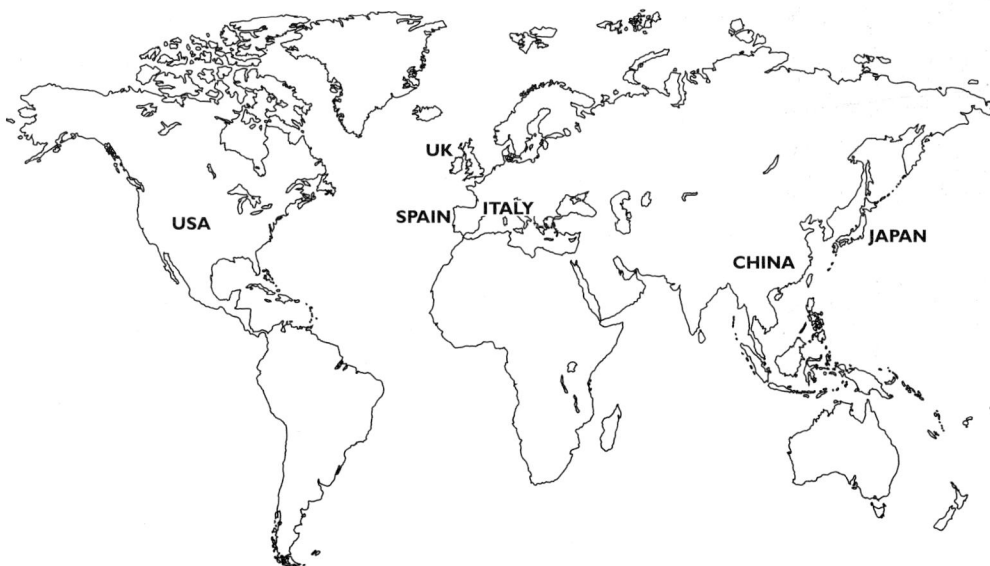

1 **Here are some recipes for traditional foods from different countries. Match the recipes with the countries on the map.**

Recipe 1
Coffee with frothy milk and a little chocolate powder on top.

Recipe 2
Rice and seaweed wrapped around some raw fish.

Recipe 3
Meat, usually beef, in a bun with fried onions and tomato sauce.

Recipe 4
Rice, fish and meat, cooked together in a special pan called a paelleria.

Recipe 5
Fried pieces of pork cooked quickly in a special pan called a wok. Served with sweet and sour sauce.

Recipe 6
A whole fish fried in batter (a milk and flour mixture). Served with fried potatoes, salt and vinegar.

2 **What are these foods or drinks called?**
How popular are they in your country?

sushi	fish and chips	hamburger	paella
	cappuccino	sweet and sour pork	

11 Open for business

Level	intermediate
Time	60 minutes
Activity	reading/problem solving/writing
In this lesson	students think of an idea for a new restaurant, bar or café and design a menu and poster to advertise it. This is a good activity to recycle all the food vocabulary that you have taught.

Teaching instructions

1 Divide the class into groups and hand out copies of the text.

2 Read out the introduction to your students and explain the exercise. Students should work through Steps 1, 2 and 3.

3 Encourage them to think of original ideas or themes for the businesses. Give them about ten minutes to work on the idea, ten minutes to think up the menu and ten minutes to work on their posters. Make sure that they've got a name and a good slogan for their business. Starting a new café or restaurant is risky. In the UK, two out of three new businesses fail in the first year!

4 When they have finished, get a spokesperson from each group to explain the idea to the class and present the poster.

5 When all of the groups have presented their ideas, get the class to vote to decide which establishment would be:

a) the most popular
b) the most profitable business
c) the least successful business

Tip - why not decorate your classroom with your students' menus and advertisements?

Many people dream of starting their own restaurant, bar or café. But it's not as easy as it might sound. A recent survey showed that two out of three new businesses fail in their first year. It often takes a lot of careful planning as well as a good idea to make your new place successful.

Food for thought

1 First decide what type of restaurant business would be most successful in your area. Think about where the restaurant will be and who the majority of your customers will probably be. For example:

fast food place	student bar
drive-in	café
ethnic food restaurant	traditional restaurant

2 Plan a typical menu of the day for your restaurant. Remember to include the prices for the food/drink/cocktails on offer.

3 Now design an advertisement for your new business. Remember to include the name of your company and try to think of a slogan to help to advertise it. For example:

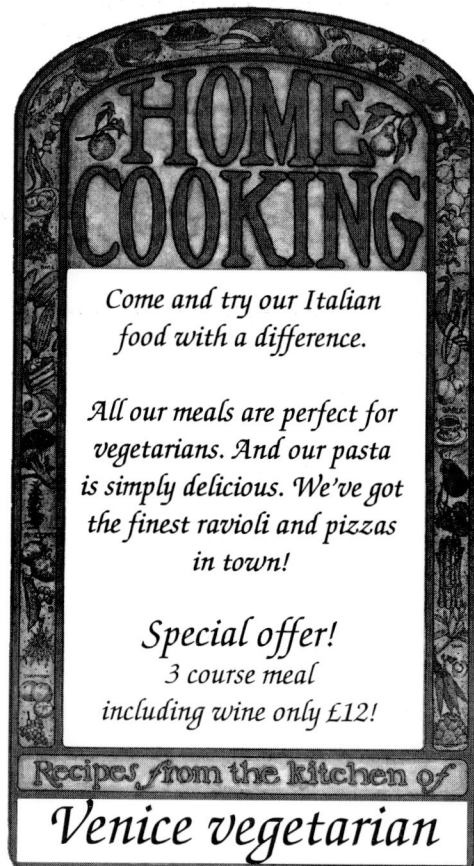

HOME COOKING

Come and try our Italian food with a difference.

All our meals are perfect for vegetarians. And our pasta is simply delicious. We've got the finest ravioli and pizzas in town!

Special offer!
3 course meal including wine only £12!

Recipes from the kitchen of

Venice vegetarian

12 Special offer

Level	intermediate+
Time	55 minutes
Activity	split reading/communication game
In this lesson	a competitive activity focuses on the language of selling. Vocabulary relating to shopping is also developed.

Teaching instructions

1 Ask your class to suggest different ways that companies use to promote their products. Write a list on the board. The list may include the following words and phrases:

   special offers   *competitions*
   new advertising campaigns   *'reward card' schemes*
   'money off' promotions   *free gifts*

2 Before your class read the texts, make sure they understand the following ideas: reward cards, collecting labels from a product and exchanging them for prizes.

3 Divide the class into pairs and give out copies of A and B.

4 Students must read their own text and then answer their partner's questions.

5 Combine the pairs to make small groups. Tell each group to make a list of three products. They can use brand names or generic terms e.g. Coke, Nike trainers or rice. Make sure that groups write their lists on separate pieces of paper.

6 Get the groups to exchange lists.

7 Tell the groups to imagine that they are advertising executives. The products on their lists are not selling very well. They must decide on a special offer to promote each of their products. They can choose from the options listed on the board. Get them to make notes on the details of each special offer.

8 When they have prepared special offers for the three products, get the groups to explain their ideas to the rest of the class.

9 Get the groups to give some feedback on each other's ideas and finally organise a class vote to choose the top three special offers.

A Gone bananas

How did a man get his local supermarket to give him 3,000 bananas and £25 for free? When Phil Calcott visited his local supermarket, the shop was running a 'reward card' scheme (where customers get points for spending money in the store). Customers collect their points and exchange them for goods. Phil was doing his weekly shopping when he spotted a special offer. 'Buy 2kg of bananas and get 25 points on your store card.' It didn't take Phil long to work out that the bananas cost £1.17, but the value of the points was £1.25. For buying the bananas, the shop would pay him 8 pence. So Phil bought every banana in the shop (over 3,000), spending over £360 and making £25 profit. There were so many bananas that Phil decided to give them away to passers-by.

Ask your partner these questions about his/her story.

1 Why are Pepsi unlucky with competitions?
2 How much did John Leonard pay?
3 How much was the plane worth?
4 Who won the court case?
5 Do you agree with the judge's decision?

Cut here ✂ -

B I claim my free plane

The drinks company Pepsi don't seem to have much luck with some of their competitions. Angry crowds in the Philippines started to riot when thousands of people won a million dollar star prize by mistake. In 1996 Pepsi ran a promotion in America where customers could collect labels from bottles and exchange them for points. For 50 points you could get a T-shirt, for 100 points you could get a rucksack, and so on. As a joke Pepsi ran a TV commercial saying that for seven million points you could get a Harrier fighter plane. Everyone thought the commercial was funny until John Leonard, a 21 year-old student from Seattle wrote Pepsi a cheque for $700,008 (enough for seven million points) and claimed his prize. The plane was worth over $24 million. When Pepsi refused to hand over the jet, John took them to court. Luckily for Pepsi, he lost the court case.

Ask your partner these questions about his/her story.

1 Why do shops have 'reward cards'?
2 What mistake did the supermarket make?
3 How did Phil take advantage of the offer?
4 How much money did Phil make?
5 What did Phil do with the bananas?

13 Take a trip!

Level	elementary
Time	60 minutes
Activity	ordering information/discussion/writing extracts
In this lesson	after revising vocabulary relating to travel, students write extracts from brochures and design holiday posters. The discussion stages revise the language of comparison.

Teaching instructions

1 Divide your class into pairs and give them a copy of Part 1. In Exercise 1 students must match the countries with their famous sights and souvenirs. When they have finished, go over the answers.

Answers

1	Turkey	The Blue Mosque	a carpet
2	Egypt	The Sphinx	a papyrus scroll
3	India	Goa Beach	some silk
4	Australia	Sidney Opera House	a boomerang
5	Spain	La Sagrada Familia	some castanets
6	Mexico	Acapulco Beach	a bottle of tequila
7	France	The Louvre	a Hermès scarf
8	Canada	Niagara Falls	a jar of maple syrup
9	Japan	Mount Fuji	a kimono
10	China	The Forbidden City	a toy panda
11	Britain	Windsor Castle	a bottle of whiskey
12	Russia	Red Square	a bottle of vodka
13	USA	The Grand Canyon	a baseball bat
14	Italy	The Basilica	a cappuccino maker

2 Combine pairs to make small groups and tell each group to work through the questions in Exercise 2.

3 Do some class feedback to find out where each group would like to go.

4 After you have done the feedback, tell the groups to write extracts from holiday brochures, advertising the places that they want to visit. Give out Part 2 as an example of what you want them to produce. The extracts should be short, approximately 80 words.

5 Each group must think of a slogan for their destination.

Variation - get students to design simple posters on large sheets of paper, with illustrations to go with their texts. When they have finished, get a spokesperson from each group to read out the extract and present their poster to the class. Organise a class vote to decide which destination is the most popular.

Part 1 1 **Match the countries with their famous sights and souvenirs.**

	Country	Place of interest	Souvenir
1	Turkey	Red Square	a toy panda
2	Egypt	The Basilica	a carpet
3	India	Mount Fuji	some silk
4	Australia	Acapulco Beach	a bottle of tequila
5	Spain	The Sphinx	some castanets
6	Mexico	The Louvre	a Hermès scarf
7	France	Windsor Castle	a baseball bat
8	Canada	Niagara Falls	a jar of maple syrup
9	Japan	Goa Beach	a bottle of whiskey
10	China	La Sagrada Familia	a bottle of vodka
11	Britain	The Blue Mosque	a cappuccino maker
12	Russia	Sidney Opera House	a kimono
13	USA	The Forbidden City	a boomerang
14	Italy	The Grand Canyon	a papyrus scroll

2 **Answer these questions.**

1 Have you ever been to any of these places?
2 Where did you go?
3 What souvenirs or gifts did you buy?
4 Add three more countries, places and souvenirs to the list above.
5 Are there any places of interest in these countries that are more famous than those listed? For example, in Britain, Big Ben and Buckingham Palace are more famous than Windsor Castle.
6 If you could visit one of these places on holiday, which would you choose?

Cut here -

Part 2

Cool Britannia

There's so much more to London than historic buildings like Buckingham Palace and Big Ben. Our history is world famous, but to be honest, these days people are more interested in London's 'cool' clubs, fantastic theatre, designer clothes and great restaurants. And if English food isn't your cup of tea, why not try Chinese, Indian or Thai? Holidays in London cost less than you think. So come to London, Europe's coolest capital.

14 Tour guides

Level	intermediate
Time	50 minutes
Activity	split reading/dialogue building
In this lesson	students will find out that being a tour guide is not easy. As well as vocabulary relating to travel, the language of apologising, taking responsibility and making excuses is also generated in this lesson.

Teaching instructions

1 Divide the class into groups of three and give each student within the group a different story.

2 Students should read their own story and tell it to the other students (with their text covered up).

3 When all the stories have been told, tell the group to exchange stories to check that they have fully understood them.

4 Tell each group to decide what they would do if they were the tour guide in each situation.

5 Here are some common English expressions connected with responsibility. Before moving on to the dialogue building section of this lesson, you might like to write some of them on the board and give examples.
For higher-level classes, try to elicit some of the phrases.

It's not my fault.
I'm sorry I can't help you.
Don't blame it on me.

It's your own fault.
I'm holding you responsible for ...

Not so fast.
It's nothing to do with me.
You should have been more careful.
You were supposed to ...
What are you going to do about it?

Which expressions are used to:

a) deny responsibility for something?
b) get someone to accept responsibility?

6 After you have gone over the vocabulary give out Part 2.

7 Tell your students to use their imaginations and prepare dialogues based on each story, writing down what they think the people might say. Explain that they have been given the first line of every dialogue.

8 When they have had about fifteen minutes to work on their dialogues, get all the groups to read out (or act out) their dialogues to the rest of the class.

Part 1

A Sick of this holiday

My company always tries to pick good hotels to stay in. Unfortunately there are sometimes disasters. During dinner a young tourist complained that his chicken tasted strange. This little boy was always complaining about the taste of foreign food. I'm a vegetarian so I didn't taste the chicken. The menu said, 'Special chicken with spicy sauce'. I told him that it was just a special sauce. The next day ten people in the group were seriously ill, including the boy. They were all suffering from food poisoning and had to be taken to hospital.

Cut here ✂ --

B Train trauma

I remember on my first tour we were going from Spain to France by train. We had to change trains at the border and we only had five minutes to do it. I got everybody off the Spanish train, with their luggage and across the platform onto the French train. I was just starting to relax when one of my tourists, a young mother with two young children, started screaming. One of her children was missing, still on the Spanish train. This was a real nightmare. Should I get off the train and leave the group to go and look for the child?

Cut here ✂ --

C Sunburn

In the Mediterranean, the sun can be really strong. You have to cover up, wear a hat and use a good sunblock when you go to the beach. Some tourists never listen to this advice. One tour guide was surprised when a woman in his group asked for help, her husband had fallen asleep on the beach. The woman wanted the guide to help her to wake her husband up. When he arrived on the beach, the poor guide realised that this was a really serious situation. The man was very badly sunburnt. His skin was red and he didn't seem to be breathing.

Cut here ✂ --

Part 2

A Sick boy's father:
'How could you allow this to happen?'

B Lost child's mother:
'Help me! Help me! I've lost my children.'

C Local policeman:
'You knew the dead man. Tell me exactly what happened.'

15 Streetwise

Level	intermediate
Time	50 minutes
Activity	exchange stories/discussion/writing tips
In this lesson	students have the opportunity to revise *should have* and *shouldn't have* in the context of difficult holiday situations. As a contrast they prepare traveller's tips, using *should* for advice.

Teaching instructions

1 Divide the class into groups of four and give each student within the group a different story.

2 Students should read their own story and tell it to the other students (with their text covered up).

3 When all the stories have been told, tell the group to exchange stories to check that they have fully understood them.

4 Tell each group to write down the mistakes that the tourists made in each situation using *should have/shouldn't have*. For example:

He shouldn't have believed the man from the airport.

5 Do some class feedback and discuss what the tourists should have done to avoid the danger in each situation. Remind the class that *should have/shouldn't have* are used to look back critically at situations in the past. *Should* itself is used to give advice. Write these sentences on the board and elicit some more examples.

a) *You've lost your wallet? You should have been more careful.*
b) *You shouldn't trust strangers.*

6 Now your class are ready for the final activity. Tell the groups to imagine that they are about to visit Killerland, the most dangerous country in the world. Get them to prepare a list of safety tips for business people or tourists visiting Killerland. Write this example on the board:

You should book taxis and pay for hotels by credit card before you enter the country because it's dangerous to take a lot of cash into Killerland.

7 Do some feedback and find out which group thought of the best advice.

A The ocean looked fantastic and the locals and tourists were enjoying themselves, walking up and down the road next to the beach. People were cycling along the beach road. Others were riding small motorcycles. My girlfriend was carrying her bag over her shoulder. I heard the noise of a motorcycle engine close behind us. Suddenly, my girlfriend shouted and I saw the motorcycle speeding off up the street. A passenger on the bike was holding a knife, and my girlfriend's bag.

Cut here ✂ --

B We were walking along in the city centre enjoying the sights. I kept my wallet in my inside jacket pocket. Suddenly a man ran up to us. He shouted, 'Sir, madam, stop! You've been robbed!' Of course, I immediately put my hand inside my jacket to check that my wallet was still there. I was relieved to find that I still had my cash. Back at the hotel, I couldn't believe it when I found out that my wallet was gone. The helpful man had watched me very carefully. He saw exactly where I kept my wallet when I checked my jacket pocket. Later he stole my money.

Cut here ✂ --

C I was walking down to the beach when a stranger came up to me and tried to shake my hand. 'Don't you remember me, my friend?' he said. I didn't recognise his face at all. 'I saw you at the airport the other day. I work there at passport control. How are you enjoying our beautiful country?' I couldn't remember him, but I was too embarrassed to tell him. He was so friendly. He even offered to take me to his uncle's seafood restaurant. We went there for dinner. The seafood was great, but the coffee did taste a little strange! Six hours later, I woke up. My money was gone and I didn't know where I was. My friend had even taken my watch and my shoes.

Cut here ✂ --

D We were in a bar when two well-dressed locals introduced themselves. When I told them that I was from London they were excited. 'You are from London? What a coincidence! My sister is going to London next week, to be a nurse in a big hospital. But she is worried about travelling to a strange country. Could you come back to my house and talk to her? She would be so grateful and my house is close to here!' They were so polite that it seemed rude for us to refuse. We left the bar and started walking to the house. Ten minutes later one of our new 'friends' pulled a knife out of his pocket. 'Give us all your money,' he said. We never met his sister.

16 Perfect parents?

Level	elementary+
Time	45 minutes
Activity	problem solving/dialogue building/role-play
In this lesson	an enjoyable activity which provides an opportunity in the role-play situations for you to work on intonation.

Teaching instructions

1 Divide the class into pairs and give out Part 1.

2 Tell the class that they have to imagine that they are parents. Get them to decide what they would do in the situations in Exercise 1 and make notes about what punishment or course of action they would recommend.

3 When they have finished, tell the groups to compare notes and in Exercise 2 find out which 'parents' are the strictest/ most tolerant.

4 Give out Part 2.

5 Students should choose two situations from Part 1 and invent dialogues to go with them. While your class are working, go round and monitor their dialogues.

6 When the groups have finished writing, get them to compare their dialogues.

7 If your students are confident, get them to act out their dialogues in front of another group; the other group must guess the situation.

Part 1

1 Imagine that you are parents. What would you do in these situations?

1 Your child wants to borrow your car for the weekend.
2 Your child wants to go on holiday with three friends from school for a week.
3 Your child wants to leave school and go to music college to study the guitar.
4 Your child wants to get married - at the age of seventeen.
5 Your child wants a new hi-fi system as a birthday present. It's very expensive.
6 Your child has decided to dye his/her hair green and have a nose ring.
7 Your child becomes vegetarian and refuses to eat with the rest of the family.
8 Your child wants to paint his/her bedroom black.
9 Your child refuses to go to university. He/she wants to travel round the world.
10 Your child fails an important exam. The teacher says that he/she is lazy.
11 Your child wants to leave home and move into his/her own flat.
12 Your child has been caught stealing CDs from a local music shop.
13 The teacher says that your child is never at school.
14 Your child doesn't want to go on holiday with the rest of the family.
15 Your child doesn't help with the housework.

2 Discuss your decisions with the other groups. Who would be the strictest parents?

Cut here ✂ --

Part 2

1 Choose two of the situations from Part 1. Imagine what parents would say to their children in that situation. Write down the conversation. For example: Your child doesn't help with the housework.

Mother: *'Jane, can you help me with the washing up?'*
Child: *'Oh Mum, can I do it later? I'm watching TV.'*
Father: *'Jane! Don't be so lazy. Get up now and help your mother!'*
Child: *'Why don't you help her?'*

2 Now act out your dialogue. Use your imagination and finish the conversation.

17 Happy families

Level	intermediate
Time	60 minutes
Activity	vocabulary building/discussion/game
In this lesson	new vocabulary, idioms and expressions about the family are introduced. The game and discussion stages also generate the language of agreement and disagreement.

Teaching instructions

1 Divide the class into small groups. Give out Part 1. Students must match the words with the definitions and fill in the gaps.

2 Help your class out with any difficult vocabulary. When they have finished the exercise, go over the answers. Make sure that the class have understood all the expressions.

Answers

1 c	2 d	3 j	4 h	5 a	6 k
7 i	8 g	9 b	10 l	11 f	12 e

3 Write the following on the board:

Things that parents say:
'This is my house and I make the rules here!'

Things that children say:
'You're always picking on me.'

4 Game: get each group to write down five things that parents might say and five things that children might say. Make sure that they write their sentences on separate slips of paper. Split the class into two teams and collect their slips. Read out the statements; the first team to correctly shout out 'child' or 'parent' gets a point. The team with the most points at the end is the winner.

5 Give out Part 2 and tell your students to discuss the statements in small groups. Do some class feedback and find out which statements the class agree with.

Part 1

Match the words with the definitions and fill in the gaps.

a) 'Like father like son'   g) sticking together
b) rota   h) takes after
c) family conference   i) gang up on
d) grounded   j) 'Act your age!'
e) homework   k) housework
f) sibling rivalry   l) blood is thicker than water

1 When the whole family meets to discuss a problem it's called a ....
2 Your parents are angry. They won't let you go out after school. You've been ....
3 Parents often say this to children. It means 'grow up'.
4 John and his Mum are so similar. He really .... her.
5 This phrase means: 'Sons take after their fathers.'
6 Jobs around the home like cleaning and washing up.
7 When two or three people get together against another person.
8 Working as one family and supporting each other whatever happens.
9 A schedule that divides the housework between people in the family.
10 Your family is more important than your friends because ....
11 When brothers or sisters are always arguing and competing with each other.
12 'You can't go out until you've finished your ....'

Cut here ✂ -

Part 2

Do you agree or disagree with these statements?

1 There's always a favourite son or daughter in every family.
2 Parents should worry about daughters more than sons.
3 The eldest child in a family should have the most responsibility.
4 There are often problems between a mother-in-law and her daughter-in-law.
5 Naughty children should be smacked; it teaches them a lesson.
6 Children always think that their parents are unfair.

18 Who are you?

Level	intermediate
Time	50 minutes
Activity	quiz/game
In this lesson	an enjoyable quiz generates the language and expressions relating to childhood. It also provides a good opportunity to practise modals of permission and ability.

Teaching instructions

1 The quiz tests your students' personalities and tries to predict whether they are the eldest, 'middle' or youngest child in their family.

2 Give each student a copy of Part 1 (the quiz). Tell them to complete the quiz individually.

3 When they have finished, divide them into small groups and hand out the analysis.

4 Groups should compare their results and find out how accurate the predictions were. Do your students agree with the comments in the analysis?

5 Part 2 practises modals of permission and ability so you might like to revise *could, couldn't, had to, didn't have to, was allowed to, wasn't allowed to,* etc. before you hand out the copies.

6 Tell your students to rewrite the sentences on a separate piece of paper, giving information about themselves when they were young.

7 Students exchange pieces of paper with the other members of the group and try to guess who is an eldest/youngest/ middle child.

8 Organise a class discussion about which type of child has the easiest childhood.

1 When you were young:

   a) you were always trying out new fashions and styles.

   b) you were always copying your brothers'/sisters' styles and fashions.

   c) you weren't interested in fashion - you were too busy.

2 When you were young:

   a) you were always fighting with your parents.

   b) you often argued with your brothers/ sisters.

   c) you didn't have many problems with your parents.

3 Your friends say you are:

   a) creative and fun-loving

   b) hard-working and responsible.

   c) good at mixing with other people.

4 If you have a problem at work:

   a) you ask other people to help you.

   b) you don't tell anyone about it but try hard to solve the problem.

   c) you try hard to solve the problem but ask other people for their advice.

5 In life:

   a) you usually get what you want.

   b) you never complain if things go wrong.

   c) you keep trying hard until you get what you want.

6 Children should:

   a) study hard and get a good job.

   b) enjoy themselves while they are young.

   c) work hard and play hard.

Cut here ✂- -

Analysis

16–30 youngest child
As the youngest child you enjoyed life, while your brothers and sisters took all of the responsibility. This means that youngest children are often creative and fun-loving, but sometimes a little selfish.

31–44 middle child
Your elder brother/sister was the leader and your younger brother/sister was the baby of the family. But who were you? This lack of identity can make 'middle' children mixed-up and quiet, or even secretive.

45–56 eldest/elder child
It's hard being the eldest child. You had to fight for your independence (staying out late, going to parties etc). This probably made you sensible, responsible and hardworking.

Score

1 a = 2   b = 6   c =10
2 a = 9   b = 6   c = 4
3 a = 2   b = 9   c = 5
4 a = 4   b = 8   c = 6
5 a = 2   b = 6   c = 8
6 a = 9   b = 2   c = 6

Cut here ✂- -

When I was a child … .

1 I could choose how to spend my allowance.

2 I couldn't stay out late.

3 I had to help my parents with the housework.

4 I didn't have to work … .

5 I wasn't allowed to borrow the car.

Part 2

19 Bewitched!

Level	elementary
Time	40 minutes
Activity	reading/speculation/writing a letter
In this lesson	the language of fear is revised while your class discuss a variety of superstitions.

Teaching instructions

1 Write the words *superstitious/superstitions* on the board and ask if anyone knows what they mean. Here are a few examples: black cats, Friday the 13th, unlucky 13, broken mirrors and not walking under ladders. All of these British superstitions are referred to in the story, so make sure that the class are familiar with them. Elicit some other examples from your/their own countries.

2 Divide the class into small groups and give out Part 1. Get your class to work through the questions and speculate about the answers. (Perhaps the neighbours moved because of 'paranormal' events next door, maybe that's why the house was so cheap; living at Number 13 might be unlucky.)

3 Elicit and then write the following words on the board:

 OK; nervous; anxious; worried; scared; frightened; terrified.

4 Give out Part 2 (Mrs Cullon's diary). Students should decide how worried they would feel in the situations she describes.

5 Tell your students to come up with 'superstitious' and 'logical' explanations for the events in the diary and compare their results with another group.

6 Extension activity: in pairs, students should imagine they are Mr and Mrs Cullon and write a letter to their neighbours complaining about what has happened.

Part 1

The day Mr and Mrs Cullon moved into their new house, an old man came to the door. 'Welcome to the village,' he said. 'I'm afraid I have some bad news for you. It's about your neighbour …' Mrs Cullon looked very surprised. They had bought the house at a bargain price, the last owners had moved to Australia. The old man told her that there was nothing to worry about as long as she liked cats and didn't mind unusual noises and smells. Mrs Cullon asked him if the neighbours were noisy. He replied, 'Noisy? Well, yes, but that's not the real problem.' He stopped for a moment to drink his coffee. Suddenly he screamed and dropped his coffee cup on the floor. 'Are you all right?' asked Mrs Cullon. The old man whispered, 'You're not a superstitious woman, are you Mrs Cullon? Good, well I'm sure that you'll be happy here at Number 13. If you want any help please come round to my house any time, during the day.'

1 How long had Mrs Cullon lived in the village?
2 Why do you think the house was so cheap?
3 Why would some people think her address is unlucky?
4 Is she superstitious?
5 Is there anything strange about her neighbours?
6 Why do you think the old man screamed?

Cut here ✂ -

Part 2   **Mrs Cullon's diary**

February

1 Sunday	8 Sunday	15 Sunday **Why is our dog terrified of the neighbour's cat?**	22 Sunday
2 Monday **Oh dear, what terrible smells from the neighbour's kitchen!**	9 Monday	16 Monday	23 Monday
3 Tuesday	10 Tuesday **The postman says that he won't deliver letters to this house.**	17 Tuesday	24 Tuesday **The neighbours were singing and screaming again last night.**
4 Wednesday	11 Wednesday	18 Wednesday	25 Wednesday
5 Thursday	12 Thursday	19 Thursday **Terrible smells again, and thousands of insects in the garden.**	26 Thursday
6 Friday **I couldn't sleep. I heard screaming all through the night.**	13 Friday **All of the mirrors in my house were broken this morning.**	20 Friday	27 Friday
7 Saturday	14 Saturday	21 Saturday	28 Saturday **My flowers are dead and the grass in my garden is black and burned.**

Level	intermediate
Time	50 minutes
Activity	vocabulary building/creative writing
In this lesson	vocabulary relating to the paranormal is introduced and practised as students write their own stories.

Teaching instructions

1 Divide the class into small groups and give out Part 1. Get your class to match the words with the definitions.

   Answers
   1 c   2 i   3 j   4 e   5 h   6 g
   7 f   8 l   9 d   10 k   11 b   12 a

2 When they have finished tell them to decide which (if any) of the 'paranormal' things might be real.

3 After you have done some group feedback, give out Part 2. Get the groups to speculate about what each chapter heading might be about.

4 Tell your students to choose a chapter heading and write a short story to go with it (approximately 100 words). They can write their stories individually or in small groups if they like.

5 While your class are working, write the following scale on the board.

   100 ⟵————————————————⟶ 0
   frightening   shocking   scary   nothing to worry about!

6 After they have had 30–40 minutes to work on their stories, go through the language on the scale and make sure that everyone understands it.

7 Get the students to tell their stories to the other groups.

8 Do some class feedback to find out how frightening the stories are (using the scale on the board).

Part 1

Match the words with the definitions.

a) possessed   e) astral travel   i) séance
b) an exorcist   f) regression   j) poltergeist
c) a witch   g) Ouija board   k) down-to-earth
d) telekinesis   h) telepathy   l) petrified

1 A woman with special powers (sometimes good but
   often bad).   ....
2 When a group of people sit round the table and try
   to contact the dead.   ....
3 This ghost is invisible and it likes to throw things
   around!   ....
4 Your body is still, but your mind leaves your body
   and travels around.   ....
5 Communication by thinking (without words or
   gestures).   ....
6 A board game where spirits spell out the answers to
   your questions.   ....
7 Under hypnosis, some people claim to have lived
   many different lives.   ....
8 When you are so frightened that you 'turn to stone',
   and you can't move.   ....
9 The power to move things around with your mind,
   (or bend spoons etc).   ....
10 A practical person who probably doesn't believe
   in magic.   ....
11 This person can make evil spirits leave your house
   or your body.   ....
12 When an evil spirit takes control of your
   body!   ....

Cut here ✂ -

Part 2

> **Welcome to *The World of the Paranormal***
>
> **Pay the reasonable price of only £12.99 and you
> can enter the world of strange, paranormal events.
> This new book tells you everything about the
> world's most mysterious unexplained events.**

**Here are some chapter headings from *The World of
the Paranormal*. What do you think the stories will
be about?**

1 My kitchen is haunted   5 Psychic police officers
2 My grandmother came   6 Friday the 13th
  back for a visit   7 Haunted by his ex-wife
3 Ouija board   8 Floating away
4 The ghostly pets

21 Unbelievable?

Level	intermediate+
Time	50 minutes
Activity	exchange stories/discussion
In this lesson	students take a critical look at various strange stories generating the language of belief and disbelief.

Teaching instructions

1 Pre-teach the following vocabulary:

  wailing noise; clinic; to cure; to wound; to spell out; telepathy.

2 Divide the class into groups of four and give each student within the group a different story.

3 Students should read their own story and tell it to the other students (with their text covered up).

4 When all the stories have been told, tell the groups to exchange stories to check that they have fully understood them.

5 Do some class feedback to find out which of the stories is the most/least believable.

6 Explain that 'sceptics' don't believe in paranormal events. Tell each group to examine the stories again, from a sceptical point of view. Get them to write short reports (100 words) presenting a logical explanation of what might be happening in each case.

7 Get the groups to compare their explanations. Which story is the hardest to explain logically?

A It was a foggy night in December and I was walking home from the pub. Suddenly I saw a ghostly, blue light in the middle of the road. It was flashing on and off, on and off, very quickly. Next I heard a loud wailing noise like a siren. I don't mind telling you that I was scared stiff. Then I saw two, tall, dark shapes moving slowly towards me. I was so frightened that I ran all the way back to my house, slammed the front door and locked it.

Cut here ✂ --

B The Imani-Liki clinic looks just like a normal hospital but none of its 'doctors' have any medical qualifications. In the clinic, the doctors all have special powers and they have already performed more than 140 successful operations by using the power of the mind! They operate by touching the patient gently with their hands and concentrating. Their special powers will then heal the patient. A wide range of medical conditions have been cured like this, including broken legs, gunshot wounds and even diseases like cancer. The hospital is so confident of success that it even offers a special 'money-back' guarantee.

Cut here ✂ --

C Over 40,000 Americans were murdered in the USA last year. Often police don't have enough information to find the murderers. So the FBI have started to use 'psychic detectives' to help. Psychic detectives use special powers like telepathy to find criminals. One example of this was a case where a man stabbed a woman in Chicago. Police officers found a glove, dropped near the scene of the crime and gave it to a psychic. After examining the glove, the psychic said that it belonged to a 30 year-old Chicago postman called David. When the police arrested the postman two weeks later, he was still carrying the knife in his jacket pocket.

Cut here ✂ --

D My friend James was getting married in three days' time so we held a party for him. Someone suggested playing with a Ouija board, a large piece of paper with the letters A-Z written on it. We sat down around the Ouija board, holding the wine-glass together. Somebody asked a question and the glass 'moved' to spell out the letters of the answer. I asked, 'Can you hear me? Is anybody there?' Then the glass moved, spelling out letters. First a 'Y' and then the letter 'E' and then 'S'. Y.E.S. spelt yes! Someone was communicating! Then someone asked, 'When is James getting married?' The board spelt out the answer: N.E.V.E.R. Three days later, James told me that his girlfriend had cancelled the wedding.

Level	elementary
Time	45 minutes
Activity	vocabulary building/making a speech
In this lesson	vocabulary relating to weddings is developed and students practise writing short speeches.

Teaching instructions

1 Write the following words on the board:

   photographs; cake; presents; ring.

   Tell your students to guess what the words have in common (they all form word partnerships with the word 'wedding').

2 Divide the class into small groups and give them five minutes to write down as many words connected with weddings and marriage as they can think of. Get them to make lists of words. (Possible vocabulary: *best man; honeymoon; the happy couple; stag party; hen party; confetti; fiancé; fiancée; bride; bridegroom; reception; engagement ring; bridesmaids; white wedding; to tie the knot.*)

3 Get the groups to compare their lists and go through any new vocabulary with the class.

4 Give out a copy of the exercise. In pairs, students must correct the mistakes in the wedding speech. Give them about ten minutes for this before you check their answers.

   Answers

1	reception/wedding	8	tie the knot
2	happy couple	9	wedding dress
3	bridegroom	10	white wedding
4	bride	11	hen night
5	best man	12	beautiful/expensive
6	wedding ring	13	wedding
7	engaged	14	Margarita

5 Tell your students that they have to make a speech at the wedding of one of the following:

   Two royal family members
   Your brother and sister
   Your best friend
   Two famous film stars
   Two famous rock/pop stars

   Explain that they can write the whole speech down or make notes, then stand up and start talking. The speeches can be made to the class or to other students in each group.

Evan is the best man at the wedding of Jordan and Margarita and he has to make a speech. Unfortunately, he's so nervous, he's got some of his lines mixed up. Correct his mistakes.

'Er, just a moment. Hello everybody and welcome to this ① *honeymoon.* I've been asked to say a few words about the ② *unhappy couple.* Of course you all know their names. Jordan is the ③ *bride* and Margarita is his beautiful new ④ *husband.* I was honoured when Jordon asked me to be his ⑤ *bridesmaid* but I was just a bit worried about losing the ⑥ *wedding photographs.* But as you can see, everything went well.

Jordan and I went to school together. He's always been a good friend, so I was very pleased when he told me that he was ⑦ *happily married* to Margarita. She's the perfect woman to ⑧ *tie the noose* with. Doesn't she look beautiful in that fantastic ⑨ *wedding cake*! She's always wanted a ⑩ *wild wedding.* And I hear that she had a great time at her ⑪ *stag party.*

I'm sure that the happy couple would like to thank all of their guests for their ⑫ *cheap* wedding presents. I'd also like to thank the hotel for the food, the florists for the flowers and most importantly you, the guests for being here for the ⑬ *funeral* of Jordan and ⑭ *Angelina.*'

Level	intermediate
Time	45 minutes
Activity	reading/dialogue building/writing
In this lesson	the students are introduced to vocabulary relating to finance and practise negotiating a fair settlement for a feuding couple.

Teaching instructions

1 Give out Part 1 and tell your students to read the text. Discuss the questions before getting the class into small groups and telling them to match the keywords (highlighted in the text) with the definitions in Part 2.

   Answers
   a) income
   b) joint account
   c) a safe bet
   d) betting shop
   e) a born loser
   f) down on his luck

2 Ask each group to decide if Belinda should leave Joe.

3 Write the following on the board:

   Joe: *Hello darling, sorry I woke you up.*
   Belinda: *Joe! Where have you been?*

4 In pairs, students should use their imaginations and continue the dialogue, writing down what the two people might say to each other.

5 When they have had about ten minutes to work on their dialogues, get all the pairs to read out (or act out) their dialogues to the rest of the class.

6 Now give out Part 3. (Just after Belinda divorces Joe, he becomes a millionaire. Now Belinda wants to share his money.) Divide the class into groups of four. Tell them to imagine that they are lawyers for Joe and Belinda. They have been told to decide how much money Belinda should get (Joe won $20 million) and how much money Joe's two children should get. Tell the groups to write down the details of their settlements.

7 Get the groups to compare their results. Which settlement was the fairest?

Part 1

Joe Hope was *a born loser*, he loved to gamble, but he never won. He bet his money on anything: horses, baseball games, soccer or boxing. The owners of the *betting shop* understood Joe's problem; he had an addictive personality and he couldn't stop gambling. It was a *safe bet* that Joe would be broke when he left the shop. Joe was always *down on his luck*, but hoping for a big win. Joe's wife Belinda also understood his personality. They had been married for seven years and they had two young children. When they first met, Joe was the perfect husband and he had a good salary from his job as a computer programmer. But soon after the wedding, Belinda noticed that their *income* was decreasing. She took a job to try to pay the bills. Then she discovered that Joe was gambling the money from their *joint account*. He was playing poker, going to the casino and visiting betting shops near his office. When she talked to him about the problem, he promised to stop. But Joe never kept his promises.

1 Is Joe addicted to gambling?
2 Why does he gamble so much?
3 Will his personality ever change?
4 Should Belinda leave Joe?

Cut here -

Part 2

Match the definitions with a keyword from the text.

a) money coming in every month   . . . .
b) a bank account for two people   . . . .
c) a bet that you are sure to win   . . . .
d) a place where you gamble money   . . . .
e) someone who has always been unlucky   . . . .
f) unlucky at the moment   . . . .

Cut here -

Part 3

'No hope' Joe wins $20 million!

He was a born loser who was always broke. But Joe Hope shocked the world today when he won the biggest prize ever on the national lottery. Joe won $20 million by choosing six lucky lottery numbers. But has the money come too late to save Joe's marriage? Last week his wife Belinda divorced him after seven years in an unhappy marriage. Money's tight for Belinda who's living with their two children in a tiny apartment. She wants half of the lottery cash as compensation for the years she wasted with Joe. But Joe swears she won't get her hands on his money. He plans to enjoy all of the cash with his new seventeen year-old girlfriend.

24 Pulp fiction

Level	intermediate
Time	45 minutes
Activity	reading/writing/story building
In this lesson	vocabulary relating to romance is developed and the activity leads to free discussion.

Teaching instructions

1 Ask if anyone has heard of 'pulp fiction'. Explain that pulp fiction describes cheap, mass-produced books like those in *The Romance Collection*, (it's also the name of a film starring John Travolta).

2 Divide the class into pairs and give out copies of A and B.

3 Students should:
   a) read their story and make sure they understand the vocabulary.
   b) cover the story up and explain it to their partner.

4 Give out the advertisement for *The Romance Collection*. Tell the students to choose the correct title for their extract.

   Answers
   A 5   B 2

5 Ask them to think of other books in the series. Write their suggestions on the board.

6 Tell the students to work in pairs and complete the final sentences from each extract.
   A When Laura walked into his room Dr Damian Stone knew that something was wrong. She whispered … .
   B James was rough, but he was so tall and dark with strong hands! She opened the window and shouted … .

7 Go round the class and get your students to read out their final sentences.

   Variation - if your class know each other quite well, get them to write their sentences on small slips of paper. Collect their answers and put them all into a hat. Draw an answer out at random and read it out to the class. Get the class to guess who wrote each answer.

8 Tell your students to choose another title from *The Romance Collection*, including any new 'titles' that are on the board. Tell them to write a short extract from that book (100–150 words). The writing can be done individually or in small groups. When they have finished, get the groups to read their stories to each other.

Tip - if your class run out of time get them to finish their stories for homework.

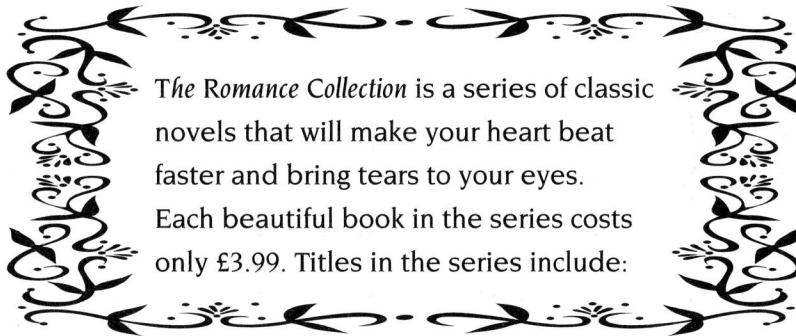

The *Romance Collection* is a series of classic novels that will make your heart beat faster and bring tears to your eyes. Each beautiful book in the series costs only £3.99. Titles in the series include:

1	*The Love Boat*
2	*The Lady Who Loved The Gardener*
3	*I Fell In Love With Her Mother*
4	Love At The Zoo
5	The Healing Hands Of Doctor Love
6	**Flight 707: On The Wings Of Love**
7	*My Heart Crashed On Wall Street*
8	I Married An Alien

Cut here ✂ -

A Thinking about Nurse Laura made Dr Damian Stone weak at the knees. The time that they spent together was so happy. But there was a problem. Damian had made two mistakes in his life. The first mistake was marrying his wife Sarah. She just didn't understand him and there was no love left in their relationship, only pain. The second mistake was more serious, but Damian didn't know about it yet. *When Laura walked into his room Dr Damian Stone knew that something was wrong. She whispered ... .*

Cut here ✂ -

B Lady Jane gazed out of her bedroom window at Rich Hall, the huge mansion near Oxford that had been the home of her family for over 300 years. Her life was so boring. She was all alone in her big house. She yawned as she looked at the green lawns and the beautiful roses in the garden. But her heart began to beat faster when she saw James, the gardener. James was a rough man, but he was so tall and dark with strong hands! *She opened the window and shouted ... .*

Level	elementary
Time	50 minutes
Activity	vocabulary building/discussion and drawing game
In this lesson	students are introduced to vocabulary relating to wildlife and the environment. The drawing activity consolidates the new vocabulary.

Teaching instructions

1   Divide the class into small groups and give out copies of Part 1. It should take students about ten minutes to finish Exercise 1. Stop them at this point and go over the answers.

   Answers
   1 c   2 d   3 a   4 b

2   Now your class is ready for the discussion statements (Exercise 2). When the groups have finished working through the statements, get them to compare their answers.

3   In Exercise 3 students have to decide whether the animals on the list are a) endangered b) not real animals c) not in danger. Give your students about ten minutes to complete the exercise before you go over the answers.

   Answers
   a)   endangered: giant panda; gorilla; white rhino; tiger.
   b)   not real animals: no eye deer (no idea); unicorn.
   c)   not in danger: brown wallaby; African lion; African elephant; sausage dog.

4   Divide the class into pairs and give out the picture strips (Part 2). Write these words on the board: *horn; fur; claws; beak; tail; scales; feathers; wings; tusks; trunk; hooves; whiskers.* Give the students five minutes to label their picture strips. Go over the answers.

5   In pairs students should design and draw their own imaginary animals, incorporating as many of the new words as possible into their pictures. Do a quick example on the board to demonstrate.

6   When they have finished their pictures, students should write a short report (80 words) describing their animal. They can do the writing in pairs or individually. The report should include the name of the animal, a physical description, details of its habitat and food, and when and why the animal died out.

7   Collect all of the pictures. Get each group to read their report to the class. Show the pictures to the class and ask them to match the picture and the report.

Part 1

1 Match the words on the left with the definitions on the right.

1	Wildlife	a)	animals that are in danger of becoming extinct
2	Global warming	b)	the place where an animal or plant normally lives
3	Endangered animals	c)	wild animals, insects, birds and fish
4	Habitat	d)	pollution causes changes in the weather

2 Do you agree or disagree with these statements?

1 People who hunt endangered animals should be sent to prison.
2 Nuclear power is good for the environment.
3 Wearing fur and testing cosmetics like shampoo on animals is wrong.
4 Testing medicines on animals is OK.
5 Global warming is a good thing - I love hot weather.
6 Companies that pollute the environment should pay the cleaning costs.

3 Are these animals:

a) endangered b) not real animals c) not in danger

1	Gorilla	5	Sausage dog	8	No eye deer
2	Brown wallaby	6	White rhino	9	African lion
3	Giant panda	7	Tiger	10	Unicorn
4	African elephant				

Cut here ✂ -

Part 2

....

....

....

Power struggle

Level	intermediate
Time	60 minutes
Activity	role-play/problem solving/discussion
In this lesson	as well as introducing vocabulary relating to the environment, this activity generates the language of agreement and disagreement and can lead to a lively debate.

Teaching instructions

1 Give out Part 1 and tell your students to read the text, explaining the history of Paradisia. Divide them into groups of three. Tell them to draw up lists of points: for and against developing tourism on the island. For example:

More tourists would improve the economy. (for)

2 Hold a mock 'public meeting' with the whole class to discuss the issue. They must vote to decide whether a new power station should be built on the island.

3 *If the class voted 'yes' to building the power station:*

Divide them into groups of three and give out copies of A, B and C.

4 Students should read their own text (about nuclear power, coal power and wind power respectively). Then they should explain the advantages and disadvantages of their type of power to the rest of the group. The process can end with a class vote, (with speeches for and against) to decide which type of power station to build. Alternatively, get the groups to write a short report, giving the reasons for their decision.

5 *If the class voted 'no' to building the power station:*

Tell them to imagine that they are members of the island's government. Even though the power station is unpopular, the government has decided to go ahead with the plan to build it. Which type of power station would the government prefer? Divide the class into groups of three and give out copies of A, B and C. Now follow the teaching instructions from Step 4 in these instructions.

Paradisia is a small island with beautiful beaches and many rare plants, fish and animals. Until 50 years ago, the people of the island lived by fishing. These days, tourism is the island's biggest industry, but many young people are unemployed and crime and drug abuse is increasing. If the island is going to develop the tourist industry it needs a new source of electricity. The old power station can't provide enough electricity for the new shops, restaurants and hotels that tourists will need.

Cut here ✂ -

A Nuclear power station

This would provide enough electric power for everything on the island. Nuclear power is cheap and it doesn't produce smoke that pollutes the environment. Lots of new jobs would be created.

but …

A nuclear power station would be very expensive to build. The country would need to get a big loan to pay for it. There's always the possibility of a nuclear accident or a radiation leak that could poison the sea.

Cut here ✂ -

B Coal power station

The old power station runs on coal which is already imported from other countries. It would be cheap to build a new coal power station. Coal power would provide enough electricity for some new hotels and shops.

but …

Burning coal already creates a lot of air pollution on the island. It is more expensive to produce electric power from coal than from nuclear energy.

The island has to import all of its coal from abroad. The price could go up.

Cut here ✂ -

C Wind power station

Wind power is very environmentally friendly and it doesn't pollute the environment. There is no chance of a dangerous accident. It's very cheap.

but …

120 windmills would have to be built to produce enough power for the island's hotels and shops.

The windmills would look ugly and they might stop tourists from visiting. It would be very expensive to build the new windmills.

Take action

Level	intermediate+
Time	60 minutes
Activity	split reading/dialogue building
In this lesson	students are introduced to the vocabulary of environmental protest and develop their own dialogues between protesters and hostile residents.

Teaching instructions

1 Before your class read the texts, make sure that they understand the following vocabulary/concepts:

   demonstrators/protesters; taking 'direct action'; to evict; reclaim; a bypass (road); locals; protest group; hippies (slang).

2 Divide the class into pairs and give out copies of A and B.

3 Students must read their own text and then answer their partner's questions.

4 When they have finished, students should exchange texts and check that they have fully understood both stories.

5 Divide the class into small groups and get them to answer the following questions:

   a) *Should people take direct action, even if it means breaking the law?*
   b) *Which story shows the most successful example of direct action?*
   c) *Do you feel strongly enough about any issues to take direct action?*

6 Tell the groups to use their imaginations to produce short dialogues between the following people (from the two texts):

   A car driver and a 'Save Our Streets' demonstrator (Text A)
   An environmental protester and a hostile local resident (Text B)

7 When they have had about 20 minutes to work on their dialogues, get all the groups to read out (or act out) their dialogues to the rest of the class.

A

Stop the traffic!

Anti-car protesters blocked one of London's main roads yesterday morning, causing long delays for drivers on their way to work. 'I think the protesters are idiots,' said one driver, staring at the group of 60 people sitting in the middle of one of London's busiest roads. 'It takes me 35 minutes to get to work by car. If I used public transport it would take over an hour and cost me three times more.' Protesters from the group 'Save our Streets' say that their main concerns are air pollution and the damage to the environment caused by building more roads. The organisation has no leaders and it relies on the Internet and word of mouth to get people to its protests. 'Everyone knows that new roads just attract more traffic,' said an activist. 'But the government never listen. Direct action is the only way to change opinion about transport. Our message is: leave your cars at home and take the train or a bus or cycle to work instead.' After a peaceful 40 minute protest, police arrived and the demonstrators agreed to move.

Ask your partner these questions.

1 How did the trouble start?
2 Where are the protesters living?
3 What is the protesters' message?
4 How much has security for the new road cost?
5 What do local people think about the protesters?

Cut here ✂ -

B

Police clash with tree people

There were violent clashes between police and environmental protesters this morning in the battle to build the Dubury bypass. About 50 protesters, living in camps and treehouses, must be evicted before the new road can be built. Demonstrators had tied themselves to the tops of trees and were refusing to move. When security guards cut down a tree, one protester fell 10 metres to the ground and was injured. Soon afterwards, fighting broke out between police and an angry crowd of about 100 people. Three police officers were later taken to hospital. So far security at Dubury has cost taxpayers £1.5 million. The protesters moved into their tents, treehouses and tunnels over a year ago. They claim that the new road will destroy a beautiful piece of countryside. 'Some of these trees are over 300 years old', said a protester. 'It's madness to destroy the environment and build a road that nobody wants.' Many locals support the protesters, but others are hostile. 'They're just a bunch of smelly hippies who are too lazy to work,' said Paul Graves, a local businessman.

Ask your partner these questions.

1 What happened yesterday morning?
2 What's the name of the protest group?
3 What's their message?
4 Why do the group use direct action?
5 What did the drivers think about the demonstrators' argument?

28 The silly season

Level	intermediate
Time	40 minutes
Activity	exchange stories/discussion
In this lesson	these strange stories generate expressions of surprise and disbelief from your students.

Teaching instructions

1   Before you give out the stories, you will need to pre-teach the following vocabulary:

   firecracker; pony; superstitious

2   Divide the class into groups of three and give each student within the group a different story.

3   Students should read their own story and tell it to the other students (with their text covered up).

4   When all the stories have been told, tell the group to exchange stories to check that they have fully understood them.

5   Give the groups five minutes to decide which stories are real and which are imaginary.

6   Explain that all of the stories were reported in various newspapers during the 'silly season'. The 'silly season' is the summer period when there isn't much going on in Britain in terms of politics and the newspapers like to print silly stories, especially about animals.

7   Now give out copies of the headlines and tell students to work in pairs within their groups. Tell them to use their imaginations and write a short story (100–150 words) based on one of the headlines (or invent a story of their own). When they have finished, get them to compare their 'silly season' stories.

   Variation - the writing activity could be set as homework.

A Pony express

A Danish man stole a pony from a field and rode it home after a night of heavy drinking. But he had a big surprise when he woke up the next morning. 'He had put the animal in a lift and taken it up to his ninth-floor flat. He had a shock when he saw the pony in his living room,' said police in Vejle, Denmark.

Cut here ✂ -

B Firework dog

Mr McMullan says that his twelve year-old dog Bruno saved his baby daughter's life. Ann was playing in the garden when some boys threw a firecracker over the fence. She was just about to pick up the firecracker when Bruno jumped up and swallowed it. There was a loud bang as the firecracker exploded and smoke came out of the dog's mouth. Although he was badly injured, Bruno survived the explosion and he's back to normal again.

Cut here ✂ -

C Raging bull

A farmer was saved by his favourite cows after being attacked by a bull. Donald Mottram, 54 was walking in his field when the angry bull attacked him from behind. It wouldn't stop kicking him and after ten minutes, the farmer thought that he was going to die. But suddenly, his cows came to the rescue. They made a circle and surrounded the farmer, stopping the bull from getting at him. 'It was amazing', said Donald. 'People say cows are stupid, but they knew what they were doing. I'm sure that they saved my life.'

Cut here ✂ -

Headlines

I   MAN GETS 2 YEAR SENTENCE FOR BITING POLICE DOG

SHEEP KILLED BY 'MYSTERY ANIMAL'   4

2   KITTEN GOES FOR A SPIN IN WASHING MACHINE

ZOO HAUNTED BY GHOSTLY CAT   5

3   INVASION OF THE KILLER FROGS

THE BIRD MAN   6

29 Sue me!

Level	intermediate
Time	50 minutes
Activity	exchange stories/communication game
In this lesson	true stories about controversial lawsuits form the basis of a discussion on legal matters. As well as building legal vocabulary this activity gives students the opportunity for free discussion.

Teaching instructions

1 Before you give out the stories, you will need to pre-teach the following vocabulary:

   to sue; to award someone compensation; fault; blame; in the wrong; incompetent; psychological trauma.

2 Make sure that your class understand the concept of suing somebody for compensation.

3 Revise some basic legal vocabulary (*judge; court; jury; evidence*, etc).

4 Divide the class into groups of five and give each student within the group a different story.

5 Students should read their own story and tell it to the other students in the group (with their text covered up).

6 When all the stories have been told, tell the group to exchange stories to check that they have fully understood them.

7 Tell the groups to decide whether they agree with the legal decisions/claims in each story.

8 Tell each group to make lists of the mistakes that people may have made in each story. Get them to make sentences for each case using *should have* and *shouldn't have* (e.g. in Text D the woman should have known that her coffee was hot).

9 If they were the jury in each case, how much compensation would they award? If the group cannot agree on a compensation figure, they can vote to decide how much money to give). Allow 15–20 minutes for them to discuss the cases.

10 Do some class feedback and get the groups to compare their settlements/reasons.

A Rugby referee

A rugby player who was badly injured in a match took the referee to court and won £1 million compensation yesterday. Dave Sheldon was a promising young rugby player, but he was badly hurt after an accident during a game last September. His doctors say that he might never walk again. Mr Sheldon blamed the referee for the accident, calling him 'incompetent'. The jury agreed and ordered the referee to pay £1 million compensation.

£1 million

Cut here ✂ -

B Drunk sues landlord

A drunken man who fell off a bar stool is suing the landlord of the pub for £100,000. Mr Roy claims that the barman should not have let him sit on the 1 metre high stool when he was drunk. 'It was all his fault. Why didn't he move me to a safer seat?' he asked in court. When Roy got drunk and fell asleep, he also fell off the stool, crashing to the floor and breaking both his legs. The case continues tomorrow.

£100,000

Cut here ✂ -

C Sue your school!

Two teenagers who failed their exams are suing their school for providing a bad education. A girl who left school without passing her exams and a boy who got low grades say it is the school's fault. They are blaming teachers at the school for their problems and they each hope to win over £30,000 in compensation.

£30,000

Cut here ✂ -

D $3 million coffee

A woman sued fast food chain McDonald's for $2.8 million because her coffee was too hot. Her doctor told the court that her mouth had been badly burnt and she had also suffered considerable psychological trauma. After an appeal, a second judge decided that $2.8 million was too much compensation and the unlucky woman only received $480,000.

$2.8 ✗ million
$480,000

Cut here ✂ -

E Extremely upset!

Courts in the USA can order big companies or rich individuals to pay millions of dollars in compensation if a jury thinks that they are in the wrong. In fact, there is no top limit to the amount of money that can be awarded. A man from San Diego was 'extremely upset' when he found a woman using the men's toilet during an Elton John pop concert. He received $5.4 million dollars in compensation.

$5.4 million

30 Scandal

Level	intermediate+
Time	50 minutes
Activity	exchange stories/writing
In this lesson	these true stories of embarrassing incidents generate the language of apologising and making excuses, and give students the opportunity of writing letters of apology.

Teaching instructions

1   Before your students read the stories, pre-teach the following vocabulary:

Chief Constable (very high ranking police officer); expulsion; MP (Member of Parliament); two-way radio; speeding; hit-and-run.

2   Divide the class into groups of four and give each student within the group a different story.

3   Students should read their own story and tell it to the other students (with their text covered up).

4   When all the stories have been told, tell the group to exchange stories to check that they have fully understood them.

5   Explain to the groups that three stories are based on real incidents and one story has been made up. Give them five minutes to guess which story is false.

Answer
D is false

6   In each story, someone has made an embarrassing mistake. Get each group to invent statements by each of the people, apologising for their mistakes (and making excuses for what they have done). In A, the Chief Constable should apologise to his fellow officers. In B, the medical student should apologise to the university. In C, the soccer player should apologise to his fans and his football club. In D, the MP should apologise to the British Prime Minister. The maximum length of each statement should be about 100 words. Students can do the writing within their groups or individually.

7   When they have finished, get the groups to compare their apology statements and discuss which excuses were the most inventive.

A   **Traffic police catch chief doing 90 m.p.h.**

A police chief was stopped by his own officers after they caught him speeding down a motorway at 90 m.p.h. A Cambridgeshire Chief Constable was stopped by traffic police on Saturday morning. He was driving his own car, south on the motorway (which has a 70 m.p.h. speed limit) at 8.50 a.m. A police spokesperson said Mr Dunne was off-duty at the time and he pulled over promptly when traffic officers signalled to him. Mr Dunne, who will have to pay a £35 fine, says that he regrets the incident.

Cut here ✂ -

B   **Student couldn't bear to fail**

A medical student who hid a two-way radio inside a teddy bear during an exam faces expulsion from a university. The 26 year-old told her friends that the toy was a good luck charm. But investigators at the University of Tübingen, Germany, say that they became suspicious when she was seen whispering into the bear's ear. The toy was later found to contain a radio which she was using to communicate with friends who were giving her the answers to exam questions.

Cut here ✂ -

C   **England soccer star smashes up restaurant**

A soccer star caught on video, throwing chairs across a restaurant was fined £4,500 yesterday and told that he was lucky not to have been given a prison sentence. The player was ordered to pay £175 to two McDonald's staff who were injured. The court saw video pictures which showed the Leeds United and England player throwing chairs at staff. He and three friends had got into an argument with the McDonald's workers shortly before the attack. The judge told the soccer star, 'This was disgraceful'.

Cut here ✂ -

D   **Drunken MP in hit-and-run shame**

An MP was in serious trouble after he admitted that he drove away after knocking over an elderly lady. Mrs Kipper, aged 72, had been crossing the road when she was hit by Piers Scott's silver Jaguar car. She suffered a broken arm in the incident. When police caught up with Scott ten minutes later, he claimed that he was 'driving to a friend's house, to get help for the injured woman'. Police stress that after a serious accident, drivers must wait until the police arrive before they can leave. Party leaders are waiting for the result of a blood test which may show that Mr Scott had been drinking.

DELTA PUBLISHING

DELTA Publishing aims to provide teachers of English - wherever they are and whatever their teaching situation - with innovative, creative, practical resource material to help them in their everyday teaching tasks.

For further information and a copy of the DELTA Publishing catalogue, please contact Eileen Fryer:

DELTA Publishing
39 Alexandra Road
Addlestone
Surrey KT15 2PQ
England

Tel: +44 (0) 1932 854776
Fax: +44 (0) 1932 849528
Email: delta@deltabooks.co.uk

Creative materials for creative teachers

ENGLISH TEACHING *professional*

ENGLISH TEACHING *professional* is an independent, quarterly magazine offering teachers of English worldwide a variety of practical, accessible, up-to-date features and articles concerned with classroom solutions and professional development.

For information on how to subscribe to ENGLISH TEACHING *professional*, please contact:

ENGLISH TEACHING *professional*
The Swan Business Centre
Fishers Lane
Chiswick
London W4 1RX
England

Tel: +44 (0) 181 995 4043
Fax: +44 (0) 181 995 1137
Email: etpemail@aol.com

If teaching English is your profession,
ENGLISH TEACHING *professional is your magazine*